Original title:
A Jungle for One

Copyright © 2025 Creative Arts Management OÜ
All rights reserved.

Author: Julian Montgomery
ISBN HARDBACK: 978-1-80581-806-9
ISBN PAPERBACK: 978-1-80581-333-0
ISBN EBOOK: 978-1-80581-806-9

The Last Fern Standing

In the midst of green and tall,
A lone fern stands proud and small.
It waves its fronds, a silly cheer,
While squirrels laugh, 'What's it doing here?'

The trees all gossip, 'What a sight!'
This fern thinks it's a real delight.
A solo act in nature's play,
With no one left to steal the fray.

A Solo Dance with Nature

In the quiet shade, I skip and prance,
With clumsy moves, I take my chance.
A snail laughs low, with a knowing grin,
Saying, 'You'll never find the win!'

Butterflies watch with fluttering glee,
As I twirl round that stubborn tree.
'Just one more twist!' I shout with glee,
But my foot gets stuck—oh, woe is me!

The Forest Within

Inside my mind, a wild spree,
Where branches grow and dance with me.
Each thought a creature, bold and spry,
That makes me giggle, oh my, oh my!

I trip on roots of wild ideas,
While mushrooms snicker off my fears.
'Take a leap,' they tease with mirth,
Into the madness of my worth!

Alone Among Giants

Among the trees, I'm just a sprite,
A tiny thing in towering sight.
With roots as thick as my wild dreams,
I dance beneath their leafy beams.

The owls just hoot, 'What's that odd sound?'
As I trip and tumble on the ground.
A solo show, in this grand expanse,
While nature chuckles at my dance!

The Hushed Heartbeat

In a world where whispers roam,
My laughter echoes, yet I'm alone.
With vines of thoughts, I climb the air,
A solo party, beyond compare.

Lurking shadows, laughing trees,
Join my madness with eerie ease.
A boisterous cheer from a feathered friend,
In this odd place, the fun won't end.

Serenade to Isolation

Banana peels slip on the ground,
Swaying palms hear not a sound.
Gorillas chuckle at my grace,
An audience for my wild embrace.

Dancing with flowers, a silly waltz,
Caterpillars wink like it's all my fault.
The solitude sings a cheeky tune,
In this solo space, I'm quite the boon.

Twisted Trunks of Thought

A lone tree juggles cloud and sun,
It's a spectacle—a twisted fun.
Sipping dew from morning's cup,
Oh, how I giggle as I hiccup!

Monkeys muse on my cringe-worthy dance,
With every stumble, I take a chance.
In the throne of leaves, I take my seat,
As laughter rings, oh this can't be beat!

Lush Embrace of Solitude

In the thicket, I twiddle my thumbs,
While corkscrew vines tangle and hum.
A breeze whispers jokes I can't resist,
Lizard laughs that simply persist.

With every rustle, a cheeky shout,
Squirrels join in—their nutty bout.
In this wacky haven, I spin and swirl,
A one-person circus in nature's whirl.

The Private Sanctuary

In my own wild domain, I reign,
Swinging on vines that tickle my brain,
Monkeys laugh at my crazy dance,
While I prance about in a leaf-clad trance.

Snakes take a nap in the sun's warm grin,
Tigers play hide-and-seek, they're quite in,
I offer a snack to a hungry crow,
He caws with delight, 'Oh, what a show!'

Leaves of Loneliness

The branches whisper secrets to the breeze,
A giraffe checks its hair; such care that frees,
My solitary hut, a cozy mess,
Filled with odd trinkets, I must confess.

Lizards practice yoga on my roof,
While frogs croak out their love and proof,
I laugh at the thought of a party tonight,
Only to find I'm the star of the sight.

Still Life Among the Beasts

A still life waits with a curious twist,
As hippos dabble in a mud bath mist,
Elephants parade with a trumpet fanfare,
While I juggle bananas with flair!

A parrot squawks, 'Where's the cake?'
I say, 'In my dreams, for goodness' sake!'
With a statue of me in the local stream,
The faunas cheer, 'What a silly scheme!'

Canopy of Dreams

Beneath the leaves, I dream in style,
A raccoon borrowed my socks for a while,
With a wink and a dance, he claims them with pride,
As I chuckle and plot my next great slide.

The stars peek in through a leafy gown,
As a lion drops in, wearing a crown,
'Where are the snacks?' he roars with a grin,
I hand him a fruit, and we both break in.

Embracing the Overgrowth

In the wild where plants all grow,
I lost my way, but enjoy the show.
Vines like snakes wrap 'round my feet,
I trip and laugh, it's quite the feat.

A butterfly flits, takes a glance,
Daring me to join the dance.
The leaves chuckle, the branches sway,
In this odd world, I'm here to play.

Solitude in the Thicket

In the thick, I've made my home,
With a lizard as my only gnome.
The sun sneaks through with golden beams,
Here, I live out my funny dreams.

I shout hello to the bumblebee,
Who buzzes back, 'You're alone, you see?'
No need for friends, or so I cheer,
The sounds of nature fill my ear.

The Whispering Leaves

Leaves whisper secrets, branches grin,
They welcome me, with wide-open chin.
A squirrel chuckles, "What brings you here?"
I shrug and say, "Just seeking cheer!"

With every rustle, a little joke,
The flowers giggle, the tall trees cloak.
In this realm, I'm never bored,
A one-person show, I can't afford!

Alone With the Monkeys

I spot a troop that swings with flair,
While I just watch without a care.
They throw me fruit, their playful ploy,
I lob it back – oh, what a joy!

One jumps close, tilting his head,
I mimic him, it's all in my stead.
Laughter erupts in the leafy air,
Who knew solitude could be such a dare?

Misfit in the Mirth

In a forest made of laughter,
I tripped on roots of glee,
The trees all wore bright banners,
Encouraging a silly spree.

The monkeys danced with grace,
While I just wobbled past,
They giggled at my clumsiness,
I'd join, but I'd fall fast.

With squirrels juggling acorns,
And birds performing plays,
I questioned my own talent,
Shouldn't I win some praise?

But in this lively chaos,
I found my groove, quite fine,
Though clumsy, I kept chuckling,
In this wild, wacky line.

The Wandering Whisper

A breeze blew soft and gentle,
Whispering secrets near,
It said, 'Watch out for critters,
Who may try to make you cheer!'

I stumbled on a puddle,
And laughed as I did splash,
The frogs croaked out a chorus,
In this fun-filled, muddy clash.

With leaves that giggled softly,
And shadows that would sway,
I danced among the whispering,
And let my worries stray.

This forest full of wonder,
Made me a curious sprite,
To find joy in the nonsense,
As day turned into night.

Embracing the Senses Alone

In the thicket of aroma,
Mangoes hung with flair,
I took a bite and noticed,
The laughter sweet in air.

The colors seemed to chuckle,
As butterflies took flight,
I chased them through the meadows,
As they danced in pure delight.

The sounds were quite amusing,
A symphony of cheer,
Each rustling leaf a giggle,
Each branch a funny seer.

I twirled amongst the chaos,
With nature's joy my guide,
In this capricious carnival,
I felt a bubbling pride.

Through a Glade of Thoughts

In a glade where musing wanders,
I tripped on tangled dreams,
The flowers chuckled softly,
As they joined my silly schemes.

Each butterfly's a mentor,
Teaching new ways to play,
They winked as I stumbled forward,
In my carefree, funny sway.

The moss beneath my footsteps,
Giggled with a squishy sound,
While shadows stretched like laughter,
As I twirled around and round.

Through thoughts that feel like mischief,
I frolicked all alone,
In this glade of whims and laughter,
I found my heart's true tone.

The Silent Treetops

High above, the branches sway,
A squirrel's chatter steals the day.
Birds debate their feathered plans,
While monkeys plot with clever hands.

A parrot squawks, oh what a sight!
He thinks he's wise, but takes to flight.
With echoes of a ticklish breeze,
The treetops giggle, oh what tease!

Solitary Pathways

I walk alone, my path so wide,
With ants in line, they won't abide.
A lizard darts, it gives a grin,
While grasshoppers play and jump within.

My footsteps thrum on squishy floors,
Who knew a leaf could hide such roars?
A toad sings loud, it cracks the hush,
And makes me laugh; I cannot rush!

Secrets of the Untrodden

In this vast green, I claim my throne,
While critters peek and laugh, I moan.
A hidden realm of slides and swings,
Each twist and turn, the joy it brings.

Beware the vines that snicker low,
They sometimes trip—a stealthy foe!
Yet vines can tickle, oh what fun,
In untamed laughter, I have won.

The Comfort of Thorns

Among the brambles, I take my seat,
Prickles hug me, what a treat!
The thorns say, 'Stay, you cannot flee,'
In spiky comfort, I feel so free.

A hedgehog wheels with crafty flair,
He rolls right by without a care.
With thorns to guard my throne so sweet,
Who knew that pain could feel so neat?

Translucent Moments of Reflection

In the wild, I trip on weeds,
Chasing shadows, not the deeds.
A parrot squawks some ancient tale,
While I'm lost, without a sail.

My only friend, a buzzing fly,
Dances near, then says goodbye.
I wave back, my heart quite light,
Caught in a giggle, what a sight!

Each tree a mirror, each leaf a laugh,
Gathering jokes on my lonely path.
The frogs croak a chorus so divine,
In this green realm, I sip my brine.

The ants are marching, in a row,
Organized chaos, what a show!
Twirling round, the breeze a tease,
I embrace the madness, with such ease.

Solitary Silhouettes

In shadows cast by moonlit beams,
I juggle thoughts, and dream my dreams.
A lone raccoon snickers at my plight,
As I tumble in the soft moonlight.

One shoe lost, the other stuck,
My antics lead to a stroke of luck.
The owls hoot and snicker low,
What a wild, silly show!

Lurking lizards offer cheers,
As I dance away my fears.
A banana peel, oh slippery fun,
In this rollicking solitude run.

With echoes of laughter in the air,
I start to sing, without a care.
My audience? A plant I found,
In my leafy realm, no one's around.

In the Heart of Solitude

Amidst the vines, I trip and roll,
The coconut stares, with a mocking soul.
Twirling around in my own delight,
While a squirrel gives me quite a fright.

With imaginations far and wide,
I ride my thoughts like a bumpy tide.
A snake hisses, but it's just a joke,
I laugh aloud, for I'm quite woke.

The sun is beaming, the rays a tease,
Tickling my toes, like a soft breeze.
Where time stands still, and fun's the game,
I and my giggles, they're both the same.

A solitary tune fills the air,
With each note danced, without a care.
Plucking petals from trees so tall,
Oh, such a merry, joyous sprawl!

The Spirit of Emptiness

In the silence, whispers sway,
Laughing leaves just join the fray.
A cactus grins, its needles bright,
Winking at me in the fading light.

The groundhog pops up to say hi,
With a little hop and a questioning eye.
Does he know I'm lost in thought?
In this green maze, fun is sought!

Mushrooms giggle, each one a clown,
Wearing caps of orange and brown.
Chasing my shadows, a game we share,
In this wise space, teasing despair.

With every tickle from the breeze,
Whimsy drapes like a soft tease.
In the depth of emptiness I find,
The greatest joys for the curious mind.

In the Wild of Oneself

Lost in a world of my own space,
Where plants have a zany embrace.
I dance with the vines, they twist and twirl,
A solo party, what a wild whirl!

The monkeys laugh at my clumsy ways,
While parrots chat in a colorful haze.
I have the stage, a solo act,
With critters around, that's a quirky pact!

The Hidden Haven

Behind the leaves, I play hide and seek,
With shadows that wiggle and softly squeak.
The mossy seats are cushioned delight,
I lounge in the shade, oh what a sight!

A squirrel's gossip tickles my ears,
As my laughter rings through the jungle cheers.
In this secret nook, I reign supreme,
An emperor of chuckles, living the dream!

Unseen Watery Meadows

In the puddles where frogs take a leap,
I mimic their jumps, my secrets to keep.
The fish giggle softly, giving a jest,
As I splash around like a curious pest!

Bamboo sticks wiggle, a bandleader's tune,
I dance with the ripples beneath the moon.
In my quirky splash zone, joy is the goal,
A watery wonderland for my soul!

Entwined in Solitude

With vines that giggle and branches that bend,
I make up stories, my best imaginary friend.
The trees sway along, in rhythm and rhyme,
Nature's own comedians, helping me mime!

The shadows play tricks, I join in the fun,
Chasing my thoughts, like a whimsical run.
A circus of one, in the heart of the wild,
Laughing with critters, forever beguiled!

The Solitary Path

In a forest where shadows creep,
I dance with squirrels, no need for sleep.
The trees all whisper, "What a sight!"
A lone explorer, out of fright.

Mossy slippers on my two feet,
I trip on roots, but life's a treat.
The birds all giggle, what a cheer,
As I tumble down, they gather near.

A one-man band in a leafy maze,
I drum on trunks in a funky craze.
With every thump, I break the day,
The wildlife joins in, hip-hip-hooray!

But when the sun begins to yawn,
I wave goodbye, my dance is gone.
A solo show, my audience small,
Yet in this green, I have it all.

Musings of a Leaf

A leaf sits high on a branch so spry,
Peeking down at clouds drifting by.
"Life's a breeze!" it giggles in glee,
"Just me and the wind, wild and free!"

Dancing round with a cheeky sway,
Swapping jokes with the sun's warm ray.
"You're all yellow, but I'm so green!"
What a party, oh what a scene!

Buzzing bees, they hum along,
A chorus here, a symphony song.
"Why do we worry?" the leaf quips loud,
"Nature's our stage; we're part of the crowd!"

But as night falls, it takes a bow,
"Tomorrow, my friends, we'll wow them somehow!"
With dreams of whirlwinds and sunny beams,
The leaf drifts down into joyful dreams.

In the Depths of Greenery

Deep in the shade where the sun can't peek,
I sip on dew, feeling quite cheeky and sleek.
The critters gossip, oh what a fun,
In this twisted maze, we all run.

Frogs play hop-scotch on lily pads,
While I crack jokes with grinning lads.
"Why did the snail cross the road?"
To get to the leaf of the cactus abode!

A party in green, with laughter and cheer,
Echoing through, in the trees we endear.
But when the shadows start to mingle,
We'll dance to the tunes of our leafy jingle.

So here I dwell, on my leafy throne,
With giggles and whispers, I'm never alone.
In this maze where the wild things strut,
Every day is a laugh, and I'm in the rut!

Portrait of a Quiet Existence

A stillness wraps around my space,
In this playful plot, I find my place.
No crowds to frighten or rush my day,
Just me and nature, in a quirky ballet.

With sloths that drift and frogs that leap,
I ponder the life of a busy bee's sweep.
"What's the rush?" I hear them say,
I'll take my time, come what may.

In this quiet nook, I hide and roam,
Crafting my thoughts from branches, I comb.
The whispers of rustling leaves conspire,
To bring me joy, my heart's true fire.

But as shadows stretch and dusk draws near,
I'll chuckle softly, no need to fear.
For in each moment, I find my jest,
In solitude's arms, I feel the best!

Wild Embers of Silence

In a forest bustling with glee,
A lone monkey dances on a tree.
He trips on a vine, oh what a sight!
He mumbles and grumbles, then takes flight.

A zebra joins in, sporting a hat,
Trying to look dignified, imagine that!
The parrot squawks, 'What a ridiculous getup!'
While the rhino just laughs, sipping from a cup.

The sun peeks through, casting shadow plays,
As creatures perform on this wild stage.
A cheetah prances with style and flair,
While a turtle just stares, beyond compare.

The jungle hums with stories untold,
Filled with antics that never get old.
In this lively mess of plant and tree,
A comical armada of jubilee!

Flashes of Solitude

A lone squirrel scampers, his stash in mind,
But oh dear, his acorns are hard to find!
He digs through the leaves, makes quite the fuss,
While a nearby sloth just rides the bus.

A chameleon changes, but not quite right,
He turns polka-dots on a stormy night.
The others chuckle, it's quite the scene,
As he tries to blend with the verdant green.

A frog croaks loudly, his voice a purr,
As he aims for a fly, oh what a stir!
He leaps and he misses, plops in the mud,
While a bird on a branch laughs with a thud.

A jaguar lounges, dressed up in style,
Wearing shades and sneakers, oh what a smile!
In this wild world of peculiar hearts,
Solitude's funny, but oh, how it sparks!

Echoes in the Thicket

In the thickets where mischief brews,
A hedgehog spins tales, wearing bright blue shoes.
He rolls and tumbles, a laugh in the air,
While a parakeet squawks, 'Where's my shiny chair?'

A bear takes a nap with a twitch of his tail,
Dreaming of honey, adventurous and pale.
His snore shakes the leaves, a thunderous roar,
While the frogs harmonize, begging for more.

A turtle plays poker beneath a tall tree,
With a crocodile who bets on a spree.
The stakes are high, but they take it in stride,
With laughter and snickers that can't be denied.

Through the thicket echoes of joy abound,
In this silly venue, pure fun is found.
Creatures convene, what a wonderful blend,
In the heart of the woods, where laughter won't end!

The Unmarred Retreat

At the edge of the woods, where the wild winds play,
A rooster decides he won't crow today.
He clucks and he flutters, what a great trick,
While the pigs roll around, getting their kicks.

An iguana, sunbathing, caught in a dream,
Thinks he's a king on a throne by the stream.
He basks in the glory of lazy affairs,
While the nearby rabbits are braiding their hairs.

A rabbit with glasses reads under the sun,
As the owls rise to say, "Let's join the fun!"
Drawing in circles, limbs and feet entwined,
This laughter-filled space keeps everyone aligned.

In this marvellous hideout, all worries suspend,
Every quirky creature, a joyful blend.
The unblemished retreat, where all can confide,
With chuckles and giggles, and dreams bona fide!

Shadows of Untamed Dreams

In the silence where whispers play,
The monkeys conduct a wild ballet.
Tigers in bowties sashay with grace,
While parrots gossip in a colorful race.

A spider spins jokes in its web of strings,
As frogs wear crowns, oh the silly things!
Lions on scooters, what a sight to see,
In this quirky realm, just the critters and me.

The leaves giggle softly, tickling the breeze,
While lizards drink tea and study the trees.
All creatures unite in this merry affair,
With laughter and cheer filling up the air.

Solitude in the Thicket

Among the vines, a chameleon grins,
Changing its hue as the laughter begins.
A sloth on a swing, oh what a delight,
Swaying in rhythm, not a care in sight.

In the quiet nook, a hedgehog does dance,
With a wig made of leaves, it takes a chance.
Squirrels in tutus join in the fun,
While out in the distance, a warthog does run.

The outfits are wild, the jokes are quite loud,
As everyone gathers, a merry crowd.
Alone in the thicket, yet never apart,
With each silly giggle, they all share a heart.

The Heart of the Wilderness

A parrot reads poems with flair,
Reciting them loudly for anyone to stare.
A gorilla in glasses, oh what a show,
Mentoring young ones on how to throw.

The turtles hold races, but take it slow,
With each tiny leap, the crowd starts to grow.
A bear shares pies, oh such a sweet treat,
While a raccoon cheers, dancing on its feet.

Jackals play games, inventing new rules,
While owls discuss the wisest of jewels.
In the heart of the wild, joy takes its stand,
With laughter and friendship, all hand in hand.

Where Silence Roams

In the stillness, a snail sings a tune,
While fireflies waltz under the moon.
The elephants juggle, trunks in the air,
With a flair for the funny, an offbeat affair.

A cactus throws shade, with a sly little grin,
While buddying up with a mischievous fin.
The whispers of crickets make giggles emerge,
As the night sky fills with a shimmering surge.

Where silence roams, the fun never ends,
With laughter and antics, all the best friends.
In the depths of the wild, amidst all the noise,
The joy of this place, oh what a smooth poise.

Whispers of Solitude

In the forest, I roam alone,
Where the bananas fight for a throne.
Chit-chat with squirrels on the side,
They think I'm nuts, I just confide.

Trees gossip about the passing breeze,
I join in, feeling quite at ease.
A parrot squawks, 'What's your goal?'
'To find my missing sock,' I extol!

A frog leaps by, but I just grin,
He jumps, I trip; oh where to begin?
Alone I stand, laughing at fate,
My only friends? The ants on a plate.

The night descends, stars dance above,
No lonely heart, just a web of love.
I whisper secrets to the night,
In this silly world, everything's light.

Echoes Beneath the Canopy

Under the leaves, I'm lost in play,
Inventing games with the bugs on display.
A grasshopper leaps right into my lap,
We giggle together, 'Well, what a trap!'

The trees sway, like they're in a dance,
I try to join, but I've no chance.
Chasing shadows, I trip on a vine,
'Who knew solitude could be so fine?'

The sound of a splat, a bird drops a snack,
I dodge it deftly, give the bird a smack.
Alone in the wild, with laughter as balm,
Even the stillness hums with calm.

I shout to the sky, 'This is my gig!'
Echoes bounce back, 'You're a funny twig!'
Amidst the wild, I find my cheer,
In this solo setting, I hold dear.

The Lonely Lianas

Swinging on vines, all by my side,
The lianas whisper, 'You're our pride!'
A sloth gives me pointers on laziness,
But I prefer laughter over stillness.

With each twist and turn, I have a laugh,
Chasing my tail like a cheerful calf.
Monkeys chuckle, they throw me a fruit,
They call me a fool, but I'm more astute.

A turtle strolls by, he takes his time,
'Don't rush,' he says, 'You'll miss the rhyme.'
I join his parade, slow and steady,
Laughing and jiving, always ready.

Even the crickets sing just for me,
Creating a tune, wild and free.
In this tangled world of joy and jest,
I march to the beat, feeling blessed.

Shadows Among the Green

In the green shadows, I make my quest,
Finding big mushrooms, who'd guess the best?
I trip on my thoughts, stumble on fun,
Even the shadows join in the run.

The ocelots laugh, they think I'm a clown,
While I shout jokes, they almost fall down.
Chirping with joy, the parrots chime,
This solitary laugh is truly sublime.

What's that? A butterfly whispers my name,
'You're the king here!' Oh, what a claim!
I twirl and I dance, feeling so light,
In this big heart, nothing feels tight.

As daylight fades, stars join the fun,
My solo adventure has just begun.
In the jungle's heart, I've found my place,
Where laughter blooms, and fears erase.

Portrait of One in Green

In the chaos, I trip and stumble,
Amidst the vines, I laugh and mumble.
A squirrel steals my snacks with glee,
Claiming the throne of this leafy spree.

The trees play peek-a-boo, oh so sly,
While a parrot squawks, 'Why not try?'
I wave my arms like a flailing fish,
In a world so wild, it's my sole wish.

Bugs join the party, a winged parade,
As I dance with shadows, a foolish charade.
A monkey snickers, with a cheeky grin,
As I tumble again, let the fun begin!

Through green horizons, I prance and bound,
In this hapless solo, pure joy is found.
With every twist, turn, and misstep,
I crown myself king, without a prep.

Uncharted Heartbeats

Beneath the canopies, I skip and sway,
As my heart beats loud, in a silly display.
The vines whisper secrets, I giggle along,
In this strange land, I'm the queen of the throng.

A bear winks as I wiggle my toes,
While sloths mock me; oh, how it goes!
I'm on a quest for the tastiest fruit,
But every misstep makes me trip in a loot.

The rhythm of leaves is a catchy tune,
With frogs as the chorus, under the moon.
I juggle my dreams while dodging a bee,
In this whimsical ballet, I'm wild and free.

Every heartthump echoes, a joyful beat,
As I chase after shadows, fate can't be beat.
With laughter as fuel, I launch into the air,
In this uncharted realm, there's magic everywhere!

Whispers of Solitude

In my quiet corner, insects hum,
While the breeze carries sounds, oh what a drum!
A lizard spies on my curious rant,
With a judgy look, I swear he can't chant.

Each rustle seems secret; what can it mean?
I ask the tall grasses, feeling quite keen.
But they only sway, like they're in on a joke,
While I trip on a root, it's no grand stroke.

The clouds overhead watch with cloudy grins,
As I prance through this mess, where no one wins.
With a twirl and a tumble, I greet the ground,
In this quiet madness, comedy is found.

Alone among echoes, I hold my own,
In this vast wild, I'm wholly grown.
Shouts of my laughter, a solo serenade,
In moments of solitude, I'm never afraid.

The Canopy of My Thoughts

Beneath the leaves, my mind takes flight,
Ideas sprout wings, they dance in delight.
A toucan scoffs at my silly schemes,
While I weave through branches of whimsical dreams.

I ponder life's choices while juggling a vine,
But all it does is tangle, oh what a line!
The ground's a soft pillow, down I fall flat,
The grass whispers, 'Welcome!' as I chat.

My thoughts are a jungle, wild and bright,
Encounters with critters ignite sheer delight.
A worm plays a tune on my wobbly limb,
While I embrace chaos, it suits me on a whim.

Each twist in the foliage, a fresh new plot,
In my tangled adventures, I tie up the knot.
What's wild is just laughter, bursting like cheer,
In the canopy of thoughts, I hold each dear.

Solitary Roots

In the woods, I dance alone,
With trees my only tone.
A squirrel laughs, it's quite absurd,
I'm ruler here, or so I've heard.

The vines sway like they know my name,
Calling me to join their game.
Yet I trip and fall, oh what a sight,
The forest giggles, day to night.

A frog croaks jokes from a bog's throne,
While I chant to the dancing stone.
"Keep your paws, I twirl with glee!"
Nature's audience just to me.

So here I sway with no regrets,
A merry king who sings duets.
Each leaf is a partner, each breeze a friend,
In my wild show, there's no need to pretend.

Wandering in the Wild

Underneath the thick tree shade,
I tiptoe to the luau parade.
Monkeys giggle, zooming by,
With coconut drinks, oh my, oh my!

A turtle winks, says 'Join the fun!'
But I'm just here to watch, not run.
Caterpillars dance, I can't keep pace,
A sneeze erupts, oh what a place!

The path is winding, leads me around,
Where mischief finds its merry ground.
Parrots squawk, "You missed the beat!"
I just grin, this groove's no cheat!

With giggles and grins, I roam at ease,
Nature's laughter sways the trees.
Are we all a part of this clownish fest?
One soul among the jungle jest.

Heartbeats of the Untamed

In the heart of chaos, I hum a tune,
With beats from a drum made of monsoon.
The critters join in, they're quite the crew,
Where vines shake low and the skies are blue.

An antelope suggests a game of chase,
But my shoes are stuck, oh what a place!
The laughter echoes through the trees,
As I wiggle and squirm, lost in the breeze.

A peacock struts in flamboyant style,
"Catch my flair!" it invites with a smile.
I spin like a top, I'm feeling so grand,
Until a banana peel slips from my hand!

From the chaos blooms joy and surprise,
As the jungle shares its goofy guise.
In this wild rhythm where nothing is sane,
I dance with the heartbeat, let go of the mundane.

Alone Among the Vines

Nestled deep in emerald maze,
I giggle at the sun's warm rays.
With each twist, new vines appear,
They whisper secrets meant for ears.

A sloth drops down to steal my hat,
I chuckle loud, "You cheeky brat!"
While a lizard plays peek-a-boo,
"Can't catch me!" it sings, "Oh boo-hoo!"

I take a seat on a mushroom stool,
Mushies say, "Stick to our rule!"
They share their snack, a tasty treat,
A banquet made for dancing feet.

So giggle with me, for solitude's fun,
I'm wild and wacky, under this sun.
In every corner, laughter thrives,
In this vine-filled world, my spirit jives!

Nestled in Foliage

In a green nook, I found my chair,
With trees playing hide-and-seek, oh beware!
Squirrels throw acorns like little snacks,
While birds giggle loud, forming their packs.

A butterfly lands on my sandwich spread,
I laugh and I sigh, I must eat instead.
The ants throw a party, all dressed in black,
My lunch now a dance floor, and I'm the snack!

Laughter erupts from a fox in the grass,
Chasing critters, he runs like a class.
I wave at the worms as they wiggle on by,
"Join me for lunch? Oh wait, never mind!"

In this wild setup, I dine like a king,
With nature's odd friends, oh the joy they bring!
From chaotically friendly to downright absurd,
My heart's made of laughter, my soul's unreserved.

Echoing Silence

In the depths of stillness, a rustle appears,
A lizard plays hide-and-seek among my fears.
A breeze whispers secrets, the trees trade their tunes,
And I'm left to wonder who's laughing at noon.

A mosquito approaches, so bold yet so small,
With a plan to outsmart me, and give me a call.
"Try if you must, but I'm quick on my feet!"
I swat the air, and my victory's sweet.

The jungle giggles, it's silent yet loud,
With echoes of nonsense that draw quite a crowd.
A toucan critiques my fashion with flair,
"Those colors, my dear, need a breath of fresh air!"

In this amusing silence, I roll on the ground,
With laughter ringing, I'm blissfully found.
A joke told by shadows, the fun rolls along,
In the quiet of chaos, I hum nature's song.

Shadows of the Forgotten

In corners unknown, where the shadows play,
Lie tales of the lost, come join in their fray.
A chattering monkey with mismatched socks,
Swings down from the branches, stealing my rocks!

An old tortoise grumbles, "Where's my grand lunch?"
He hiccups quite loud, all set for a munch.
The shadows all giggle, gathering near,
With whispers of silliness that fill the air.

An owl gives me winks from its perch overhead,
"Your snacks, my dear friend, would go well with bread!"

A dance with the ferns, we sway to the light,
The forgotten shadows, they're fun every night!

With madness and mirth, the dark sing their songs,
In laughter and giggles, where nothing feels wrong.
In the shadows so wild where lost hopes can dart,
I find all the humor that lives in my heart.

The Sway of Solitude

Alone in the wild, with a cheeky grin,
I shimmy with branches and dance with the wind.
A parrot comments on my awkward flair,
"Your moves need some rhythm; might I give you air?"

In my private groove, the frogs start to croak,
Their chorus so odd, I can't help but choke.
With each little leap, they jump into sight,
Joining my party, oh what a delight!

Through the twisty paths, I spin with delight,
The solitude boasts a whimsical flight.
The trees seem to giggle, their leaves in a whirl,
As I shuffle and jiggle, losing my world.

In this land of misfits, I twirl all around,
With laughter erupting, my joy knows no bound.
Embrace the sweet quiet, dance wild and free,
In solitude's sway, I find joy simply me!

Melodies of a Hidden Glade

In a leafy room where shadows play,
A lone sloth sings, in a lazy way.
The frogs join in with croaks and croons,
While squirrels dance under bright, round moons.

A parrot jokes with a toucan friend,
Telling tall tales that never end.
The breeze, it chuckles through branches green,
In this hidden glade, a funny scene.

The bumblebees buzz a melody sweet,
While turtles trip on their tiny feet.
An orchestra plays with leaves as the score,
Who knew the wild could mean so much more?

A vine swings low, and a monkey slips,
He lands with a thud, and everybody quips.
In the heart of the fun, away from the light,
This merry band thrives, from day to night.

In the Embrace of Foliage

Under the ferns, something stirs and shakes,
A hedgehog races, oh, what a faux pas!
He bumps the toad, who lets out a croak,
Together they tumble—oh, that's no joke!

The wise old owl hoots with glee,
While munching leaves from a nearby tree.
A snake slides by, doing the twist,
With a wink and a nod, he can't be missed.

A squirrel tries juggling acorns with flair,
But slips on a leaf, oh, who would dare!
The laughter echoes through the thick boughs,
As mischief abounds in the leafy house.

The shadows dance as the sun starts to dip,
In this leafy embrace, life's quite the trip!
From clumsy critters to silly spills,
Nature's comedians, giving us thrills.

The Solitary Stream

A trickling stream with a wink and a wave,
Carries a snail who's feeling quite brave.
He flips on his back, then spins like a top,
While minnows giggle and give a small hop.

A frog with a crown jumps high on a log,
Singing a tune, making fun of the fog.
The fish swish and sway, shaking their tails,
Betting on who will win the next trails.

A wise old turtle rolls by with a grin,
"What's wrong with a splash? Let the fun begin!"
The water splashes, and all creatures cheer,
In this trickling show, nothing to fear.

So come take a dip in the glimmering light,
Where laughter flows freely, from morning to night.
The solitary stream, a comedy stage,
Where each ripple tells tales, a funny page.

Echoes of Untamed Dreams

Deep in the woods where wild dreams collide,
A raccoon, in mischief, takes great pride.
He tips over trash bins with a silly flair,
Leaving a trail of confusion everywhere.

The deer join in, prancing about,
Playing tag with shadows, laughing out loud.
While chipmunks chit-chat, quite the debate,
On who has the best stash, oh, isn't it great?

An echoing chorus of giggles and grunts,
Sings through the forest, oh, what silly fronts!
Each critter with tales, from great to absurd,
In their wild summits, their voices are heard.

So come take a stroll through this funny parade,
Where untamed dreams lead the way, unafraid.
With laughter and antics, the wild comes alive,
In this radiant realm, where joy will thrive.

Selves Revealed in Shade

In the thicket, a monkey swings,
Wearing my hat and those ridiculous things.
He grins wide, quite the fashionista,
Stealing my snacks, a true prankster.

A sloth prowls, dressed in a cape,
Claiming to be a superhero, with no escape.
He takes naps mid-mission, it's quite a sight,
Declaring his powers when he feels just right.

Elephants are picking up my lost shoes,
With trunks raised high, they've got the clues.
They trumpet a tune, my feet trapped in flair,
Dancing around, revealing their care.

Yet here I sit, laughing with glee,
In this company of beasts so free.
Their antics remind me, life's never bland,
When you find fun in the wild, make a stand.

Journey of the Lonely Traveler

Wanderer lost in the tangled vines,
Swap my compass for silly signs.
A parrot squawks, gives me directions,
Fails to mention my misperceptions.

Tripped by roots, I fall with a thud,
Laughter echoes, it's not all so crud.
A turtle jogs by, moving quite slow,
Says, "Hurry up! It's time for a show!"

I share my snacks, and they come in waves,
An audience of critters, oh how it misbehaves!
A dance-off breaks out, with a cat in a hat,
While I sip my drink, feeling less flat.

As night falls on this quirky scene,
With fireflies waltzing, it's quite the scene.
A buddy I've found in path and in plight,
On this odd journey, everything's light.

Lurking Shadows of the Mind

In corners dark, where fears conspire,
I see dancing shadows, a laugh to inspire.
A ghost dressed as me, with a cheeky grin,
Says, "Join the fun, let the madness begin!"

He flips through my memories, one by one,
Turning my frowns into a pun-filled run.
Together we juggle my past with a cheer,
Each thought a balloon, ballooning with fear.

We dance in the twilight, not caring to hide,
With laughter that echoes, nowhere to bide.
My shadows are silly, my worries outdone,
Finding humor in each, we play till it's done.

Each fear that once loomed now giggles and jumps,
Joined by a chorus of silly little clumps.
In this strange dance, my heart starts to glow,
Lurking shadows become friends in tow.

Roots of Reflection

Stumbling on roots that twist and twine,
Can't help but laugh at the mess that's mine.
I try to dig deep, for wisdom to gain,
Instead a chipmunk squeaks, "Worry's a pain!"

In the mirror of leaves, I glimpse some surprise,
A walrus with eyebrows, wearing cloud disguise.
He blinks at me, then begins to recite,
"Life's all a circus, so join in the plight!"

Interviewing blooms, those chatty odd folks,
Whispering secrets and sharing their jokes.
The blooms giggle wildly, with petals unfurled,
A party of thoughts, oh, what a world!

Reflecting on roots that lead underground,
I find that in laughter, true treasures are found.
So here's to the quirks, the grins that unfold,
In this garden of madness, life's story is told.

Swaying Alone Between Shadows

In the canopy high, the leaves chatter,
A squirrel thinks I'm nuts, what's the matter?
I sway with a vine, a dance so bold,
But only the parrot finds it gold.

A frog in a pond croaks jokes all day,
I laugh at the ripples, the funny way.
The branches wiggle, the flowers tease,
Do they giggle at me, or just the breeze?

Bamboo is bending, it laughs at my plight,
I'm the star of the show, in nature's light.
With shadows for friends, I'm never alone,
Who needs a party? I'm the king on my throne.

A snake slithers by, with a wink and a grin,
"Hey buddy, you danced? Where to begin?"
I laugh as I dodge, in this wild overgrown,
With laughter and vines, I've happily grown.

Beneath the Solitary Sky

Under a driftwood, I sit and I muse,
A bird on a branch gives me funny news.
The clouds above puff, they're all dressed in white,
Making silly shapes in the fading light.

An ant crawls along, with a grand little plan,
"Why walk so slow, when you can run, man?"
I cheer from my seat, "You're a champion tonight!
Let's race for the crumbs, it'll be a delight!"

The rain drops down, and I spin like a top,
Each droplet's a friend, I'll never say stop.
"I'm no hermit!" I shout to the buzzing bees,
Who hum my name like they're tickling the trees.

When the stars pop out, it's a wild, wild show,
I kick up my feet, let the moonlight glow.
In this big open space, I laugh loud and clear,
A solo soiree, with my friends gathered near.

Serene Isolation in Green

In the heart of the woods, I grinned with delight,
A raccoon waved at me, "Oh, what a sight!"
He rummaged for snacks while I danced on a log,
"Join in my party!" I called to the frog.

The shadows all chuckled, the flowers swayed too,
"I'm alone but not lonely!" I shouted, "How about you?"
A breeze whispered secrets, tickling my face,
I giggled at shadows, and fell, what a chase!

The trees stretched their limbs, like they're ready to play,
"Come join us, oh dweller, your worries away!"
So I joined in their game, we spun 'til we fell,
In a giggling heap, oh, this laughter's a spell!

In solitude's arms, I find joy everywhere,
Every rustle and wiggle, it tickles the air.
Who needs a wild crowd? Nature's my throne,
I sway with my pals, in this world all my own.

Forgotten Pathways

Along the old trails, where the wildflowers bloom,
I twirl like a dervish, making my room.
A butterfly flutters, and does a quick spin,
"Dance with me, friend, let the fun times begin!"

An old stone talks back, with a mossy intent,
"Life's a silly story, with fun time well spent!"
I chuckle at ferns as they sway to their song,
They bend and they weave, come join in along!

Past the tangled roots, where the ants have their fun,
They march in formation, their work never done.
I wave them hello, as they march to their beat,
In this wild little world, every moment's a treat.

As twilight descends, it's a riot of cheer,
With fireflies blinking, as if drawing near.
So here on this path, I find joy every hour,
In laughter and light, I'm a sole blooming flower.

Whispers Beneath the Canopy

In the depths of green, I find my place,
Where leaves giggle and tickle my face.
A squirrel jokes and winks at me,
I laugh with shadows, wild and free.

The vines twist like a funny mustache,
While vines dance slow, I make a splash.
The parrot squawks a pun or two,
Even the bugs have gags to chew.

A sloth in pajamas, takes a snooze,
While monkeys swing, without a bruise.
Each branch a stage, each rustle a cheer,
I'm the star in this leafy sphere.

With each chirp and chortle, I spin and sway,
In my own little world, come what may.
A symphony of laughs so keen,
In this green paradise, I'm the queen!

Reflections from a Hollow Tree

I sit in a trunk so wide and grand,
Listening to owls who misread the band.
'Who-who's the wisest?' they cackle with glee,
While I'm the thinker, sipping my tea.

Raccoons stage plays with flair and fright,
Dressed as bandits, under moonlight.
The beetles are the critics, quick to critique,
Bumbling words, but what do they seek?

Branches creak under the weight of my dreams,
As squirrels draw plans in wide expert schemes.
Each rustle a riddle, each flutter a song,
In this hollowed retreat, I've belonged all along.

With frogs as my chorus, croaky and loud,
I reveal my secrets to the quiet crowd.
I chuckle to spirits, both raucous and shy,
In this cozy tree hollow, time passes by.

Last Traveler in the Thicket

In a patch of green, I wander and roam,
The wild wild weeds, they call me home.
A lizard offers directions with flair,
But who's the last traveler? I'm quite unaware.

With thorns for friends and twigs for my chair,
I share all my stories, with a dash of despair.
The breeze whispers secrets, tickles my ears,
While butterflies flutter, confirming my fears.

I stumble on roots that trip with delight,
And giggle with vines that tangle just right.
A hedgehog quips, "Hey, don't be forlorn!
You're the last one here, let's laugh till we're worn!"

Through brambles of giggles and puddles of fun,
I leap and I tumble, oh, what a run!
In the thicket I find joy's sweet embrace,
As the last traveler, I've truly found grace.

Solitary Murmurs

In the jungle alone, I bubble and bounce,
Blowing up giggles as I quietly pounce.
The ferns gossip softly, in code about me,
While I plot my stand-up, can't wait to be free.

A caterpillar runs a marathon now,
While I cheer from the sidelines—"Take a bow!"
Gosling hears whispers, ducks flap about,
In a world of oddities, I'm sparking a shout.

The crickets join in with their fiddly tunes,
While I'm deep in the brush, acting like a loon.
Roots trip my feet, laughing at my plight,
The crumbles of joy linger deep in the night.

I craft a solo show, where I'm the star,
In a mossy theater, no need to go far.
With chuckles and murmurs, I dance on my own,
In this land of laughter, I've never felt alone.

Echoes of Green Isolation

In the wilds where shadows creep,
A lizard sings while I just sleep.
A monkey laughs, my only friend,
In this space where sounds don't end.

The birds all chirp, but do they know?
I'm the king of my own show.
With every rustle, I turn around,
Is that a ghost I've finally found?

The vines above begin to sway,
Dancing to songs they've made from clay.
I share my jokes with the breeze,
It laughs so hard, it starts to wheeze.

In this chaos, I feel divine,
A solo act without a line.
The trees, they offer me no cheer,
But I between them, shine sincere.

Solitary Vines

With roots that twist and turn just right,
I stumble through my leafy fright.
The brambles tickle at my toes,
In the thicket where nobody goes.

I find a frog that croaks a tune,
As if he knows I'm here at noon.
He closes one eye, takes a leap,
And all my secrets he will keep.

A squirrel watches with lots of glee,
He plays peekaboo right up a tree.
I shout a joke but he just squirms,
I guess my humor's out of terms.

The vines above hang tight with grace,
Making this my favorite space.
Alone I thrive, I'm on my own,
In wild absurdity I've grown.

Secrets Beneath the Leaves

In shadows where the critters glow,
I hear the whispers, soft and slow.
A turtle tells me what's left unsaid,
His wisdom stirs beneath my head.

With beetles forming marching bands,
They parade around with tiny hands.
But when I wave, they all just flee,
Guess they don't dance with a me.

The leaves above are thick and lush,
While down below, the creatures hush.
I try and laugh, but no one stays,
Just me, my thoughts, and leafy rays.

The follies of this leafy dance,
Paint my solitude in vibrant chance.
With nature's quirks, I find my cheer,
In secrets' depths, I thrive right here.

A Lonesome Symphony

The rustle of leaves, my only sound,
In a symphony where I'm the crowned.
A bat performs its midnight flight,
While I compose beneath the night.

A stray cat hums a solo song,
It prances by where I belong.
With each pounce, it claims the ground,
While I just chuckle, blissfully bound.

The owls hoot what they've overheard,
But the echo is absurdly blurred.
When I try to hum along in tune,
The frogs just croak and end too soon.

Each note I find on this wild stage,
Is laughter wrapped up in every page.
And though I'm here without a crowd,
I make noise, and sing out loud!

Guardians of the Solitary

In the depths where the wild things play,
A lone tiger lounges all day.
He thinks he's the king of the lot,
But he's just a big cat seeking a spot.

The monkeys swing high, trying to tease,
While the tiger just dreams of a soft, warm breeze.
He chases their tails, they giggle and flee,
This jungle's a mess when it's just you and me.

An elephant saunters, tripping on vines,
He steps on a snake who's plotting designs.
"I heard you're outnumbered!" the serpent will hiss,
But one silly stumble ends all of this bliss.

So gather your friends or the funny brigade,
In the jungle of laughter, jokes never fade.
Where each little mishap leads to a grin,
In this silly wild life, we're all meant to win.

The Hidden Retreat

A leafy retreat where I bumble and prance,
I trip over roots as I start my dance.
With squirrels as partners, I twirl and I spin,
Each stumble a victory, a laugh from within.

In my secret hideout, I chomp on a treat,
A stash full of berries, oh what a feat!
The parrot squawks loudly, "Is that pie on your face?"
I wink and I laugh, it's my favorite place.

The vines start to tangle, a twist and a knot,
I make it a game; I'm tangled, I'm caught.
A frog leaps beside me, gigging with glee,
He croaks, "At this rate, you'll invite a tree!"

So I chuckle and stretch, let the silliness flow,
In this hidden oasis, where laughter will grow.
No worries, no troubles, just pure, wild fun,
In my secret jungle, I'll always run.

Through the Eyes of the Wanderer

I wander through thickets, so green and so bright,
With shrubs that sing songs, what a delightful sight!
The critters all stare as I trip on a vine,
"Hey, watch that step, are you doing just fine?"

An owl gives me wisdom, "You've lost your new hat!"
While a turtle smiles slowly, "Just look where you're at!"

I laugh at their banter, so goofy and wise,
Who knew jungle critters were such funny guys?

The glade opens up, and the sunlight spills down,
I spot a lost sock, strung out like a clown.
The monkeys go crazy, they're ready for fun,
"We'll start a new fashion!" they screech, "Come on, run!"

So off we all go, with a sock on my head,
In a world where the laughter will never be shed.
With friends all around me, the vibe feels just right,
In the eyes of this wanderer, joy takes its flight.

Life Among the Shadows

In the quietest corner, the shadows do play,
While I sip on some nectar, filling my day.
A beetle winks by, "Careful not to spill,
Or you'll wake the big dad, he sleeps by the hill!"

The frogs croak a tune, a bizarre serenade,
While I twirl with delight, in this craftily laid glade.
But wait, what is this? A rustle, a thump!
A clumsy old sloth gives a woeful little jump!

He grumbles and gripes about how time's too slow,
"I'd be quicker, you see, if my belly didn't grow!"
And all of the critters begin to agree,
This life of mischief is also carefree.

So let's lead our lives without worry or fear,
In shadows of laughter, let's gather near.
For in this wild world, with quirks that abound,
Life among the shadows is the best, joy is found.

Venturing Into Solitude

In a jungle of vines, I roam around,
Talking to parrots that mimic my sound.
I slip on a vine, fall flat on my face,
The monkeys just laugh at my comical grace.

With a lion-sized snack, I work on my tan,
While a meerkat plans out a real-bandit plan.
A snake gives a wink, says, "You're the best!"
I salute with my sandwich, feeling quite blessed.

The frogs throw a rave, to my own surprise,
With glow-in-the-dark flies buzzing through skies.
Dancing barefoot on moss, what joy can be found!
Next thing I know, I'm lost on the ground.

I sip on a coconut, pondering eyes,
At the sloths giving hugs—what a slow surprise!
Perhaps I'll embrace this odd solo quest,
In this quirky life, I might just be blessed.

Solstice of the Single Heart

Beneath the tall trees, the shadows grow long,
I sing to the crickets; disguise my wrong song.
A toucan joins in with a loud honk and grin,
As the squirrels cheer on my Solstice win.

A hammock swings wildly as I take a rest,
With bugs playing games in my soft summer nest.
My fruit salad falls—oh, what a grand mess!
I sprinkle some laughter and call it success!

When a parrot drops jokes, it's a real slapstick,
I chuckle so hard, it's a magical trick.
The sun dips down low, and the fireflies glow,
With laughter resounding like nightly encore.

I toast to the stars, my celestial friends,
Content in this solitude, it never ends.
I'm wrapped in my blanket of giggles and cheer,
In this vibrant place, I'm as free as a deer.

A Private Oasis

In a hidden cove, I've made quite the splash,
With an inflatable flamingo, I make a grand crash.
Goldfish swim by, giving me the eye,
And I can't help but giggle; it's just my style.

The sun makes a toast to my silly wit,
While the clouds sit back, watch me play and commit.
I crown a pineapple king of my land,
With a juice box throne, oh, isn't it grand?

Though no one can see me, I wave from my chair,
To the bees who buzz by, without any care.
The drumming of raindrops forms a beat on my shell,
As I dance with the rhythm; I know it so well.

The waves play along with my whimsical dreams,
While the sun paints the sky in vibrant sunbeams.
Here in my oasis, the laughter feels bright,
In a world all my own, everything feels right.

Solitary Echoes

In a forest so deep, my thoughts start to hum,
Echoes of nonsense emerge with a drum.
A fox gives a nod as we share the same strife,
With a wink, he declares, "This is the good life!"

Under trees, I sip tea with ants in a row,
As the flowers debate which way they will grow.
A wise old owl tells me stories of fame,
I laugh at the thought, as he calls out my name.

I challenge the shadows to dance through the night,
While the fireflies twinkle, a magical sight.
The raccoons bring snacks; oh, what a delight!
When solitude's funky, there's no need for fright.

So here in my space, I embrace the unknown,
With critters and giggles, I feel right at home.
In echoes of laughter, I truly belong,
In this peculiar world, life feels like a song.

Lost in the Ferns

In the midst of ferns so wide,
I tripped over a turtle's ride.
Running in circles, feet in a dance,
Chasing shadows, not a chance!

Suddenly a parrot squawked,
"Watch where you're going, or you'll be locked!"
I laughed so hard, fell on my back,
The turtle chuckled, got me on track.

Through the leaves, I met a goat,
Who wore a hat and sang a note.
With every bleat, he told a tale,
Of silly walks and goldfish sail.

Then a monkey swung, a cheeky fellow,
Taught me laughter, bright and yellow.
In ferns I roamed, my heart so light,
A wild adventure, pure delight!

The Quiet Grove

In a grove where whispers play,
I found a frog who liked to sway.
He croaked a tune, so out of place,
A dance-off with a smiling face.

The trees giggled as I joined in,
Tripping over roots and grinning big.
A squirrel threw acorns, aiming high,
I ducked and laughed – oh my, oh my!

A wise old owl with glasses perched,
Declared, "This dance, it needs some church!"
So we formed a conga line, absurd,
Dancing 'round without a word!

The grove was alive with joy and sound,
Where giggles and folly did abound.
As the sun began to set low,
I knew this place would steal the show!

Solace in the Wild

In the wild, a cat in a crown,
Declared she'd rule, never a frown.
With a swish of her tail, she held court,
Gathering pals for a jolly sport.

A chameleon, with colors bright,
Changed a hue with each new plight.
He joked about style, oh so chic,
While a sloth cheered, "I can't take a peek!"

Under branches, the laughter grew,
As a bear tried to fit in a shoe.
He stumbled and fell with a hefty thud,
While ants threw a party in the mud!

We basked in shade, a merry band,
With stories tall and hearts so grand.
Amongst the wild, we found our glee,
A motley crew, just you and me!

Reflections in a Leaf

A leaf as a mirror, I gazed in grace,
Saw a funny face, I couldn't erase.
It winked back at me, playful and bold,
In the heart of the green, my spirit extolled.

The trees held whispers, secrets so dear,
I chuckled at squirrels, hoarding with cheer.
Each nut in their stash, a treasure they claim,
"Let's split them all!" was their silly game.

Got lost in the shadows, caught in a whirl,
As a beetle taught me an awkward twirl.
With wiggly legs, he claimed to be slick,
While I tried hard not to trip and stick!

So in the leaf, my laughter soared,
All in the forest, where jokes are stored.
A funny world, a wondrous sight,
Reflections of joy, oh what a delight!

Encounter with the Unknown

In a forest thick, I took a stroll,
Where trees wore hats, and squirrels were bold.
A porcupine winked, oh what a sight,
As I wondered about my newfound fright.

A chattering monkey swung by my ear,
Inviting me in for a raucous cheer.
He danced on the branches, a silly spree,
While I laughed and guessed what his name could be.

Suddenly there rose a loud, funny roar,
I turned to see a lion, looking for more.
He tripped on a vine, oh, what a blunder,
And in that moment, I couldn't help but wonder.

With giggles and grins, my day went awry,
In this wild circus, I wished I could fly.
Each creature a tease, in this vibrant abode,
Adventures galore, down a chuckling road.

An Intimate Wild

Beneath twisted boughs, I met my new mates,
A turtle with glasses, debating his fate.
He spoke of the stars and a world so wide,
As I chuckled at thoughts of a slow-motion ride.

In a patch of green, a deer shared a joke,
About a lost shoe and a mischievous oak.
With laughter so bright, we reveled in fun,
Who knew that a forest could offer such sun?

A raccoon peeped through the bushes with glee,
With a sack full of treasures, just him and me.
We planned a big feast of fruit from the trees,
While squirrels looked on, ignoring the breeze.

As the critters gathered, we danced in delight,
Under moonbeams that shimmered all through the night.
With joy in the air and snacks on the side,
This intimate wild, where all creatures abide.

Pondering Beneath the Shade

In the cool of the shade, I sat for a while,
A parrot squawked laughter, my heart wore a smile.
He told me of pirates, of treasure and gold,
As I sipped on a fruit drink, feeling bold.

Near a brook bubbling softly, a frog joined the chat,
He leaped for a fly and fell flat with a splat.
We roared with laughter at the sight so absurd,
As the parrot just squawked, 'I was watching, you nerd!'

While pondering life, a wise old raccoon,
Said, 'Why worry, my friend? Just dance to your tune!'
With a wink and a jig, he made my heart soar,
In this playful oasis, who could ask for more?

So I lounged in the shade, with friends bright and keen,
In a jungle of laughter, where the joy was supreme.
Where simplicity thrived and fun was the aim,
Each moment a treasure, no two quite the same.

Tangle of My Mind

Lost in my thoughts, like vines on a tree,
A monkey approached, with a grin just for me.
He juggled some nuts, then fell on his side,
Laughing so hard, it was tough to hide.

With each poke of a stick, my worries got lost,
As a chipmunk suggested, 'Find joy at all cost!'
He built a small pyramid of leaves and of twigs,
And while we all marveled, began to do jigs.

The vines seemed to whisper, with secrets to share,
In this tangled-up world, free from worry and care.
We danced in the sun, letting worries unwind,
As I laughed at the chaos, a tangle of mind.

And as the day wove its colorful thread,
The critters agreed, life was better instead.
So join in the folly, don't take it too serious,
In this fun little jungle, everything's mysterious.

The Solace of Stillness

In the thick of the trees, I found my shoe,
A pair of eyes blinked, then off it flew.
I laughed to myself, what a sneaky thief,
A squirrel with style, beyond belief!

The breeze tickles leaves, they dance on a whim,
A chubby raccoon joins with a cheeky grin.
He weights the scales, a fuzzy, bright blunder,
Foraging snacks, it's a true food wonder!

Sunlight peeks through, casting silly shadows,
A butterfly flutters, chaos follows.
An ant in a suit, with a leaf for a hat,
Marches in line, oh, where's he at?

Laughter echoes, birds join the spree,
Nature's own circus, it's just for me.
On this wild stage, I'm the sole guest,
In my own little world, I'm simply a pest.

A Hidden Wound

A vine came a creeping, oh what a sight,
Its grip on my ankle gave me a fright.
I stumbled and tumbled, kissed a big tree,
Nature's clumsy joke, how it tickled me!

The plants giggle softly, trees snicker in glee,
A bird spots my blunder, it's all so carefree.
With feathers that shimmer, it chirps and it dives,
I'm the star of the show that nature contrives.

A nearby frog croaks, "What a charade!"
I respond with a grin, and I'm not dismayed.
With mud on my shoes and leaves in my hair,
I'm the king of this mess, without a single care.

I take a deep breath, let the laughter take hold,
The jungle has secrets, but oh, they're bold.
Each trip and each tumble, a lesson in fun,
In this tangled bliss, I'm never outdone.

The Quiet Grove

In the calm of the grove, I've lost my way,
A mockingbird laughs, "You'll be here all day!"
With branches a-snicker, and sunlight a-glow,
I'm the wandering fool that no one should know.

A chipmunk in striped pants takes a grand stand,
He challenges squirrels, "I'm the best in the land!"
As I sit back and watch this odd little show,
I can't help but chuckle; this place is aglow.

The grasses are swaying, with giggles anew,
They tickle my toes, like the friendly boo.
With butterflies swirling like confetti in air,
I join in the dance, with my goofy flair.

So here in this haven, with laughter and cheer,
I savor the antics of nature so dear.
Each moment a treasure, a whimsical tale,
In this playful grove, no one's bound to fail.

Boundless Solitude

In solitude's arms, I trip on a vine,
The laughter of crickets, it's truly divine.
I twirl with the ferns, a dance all my own,
In the company of dew, I'm never alone.

A sloth with a swagger, so slow and so proud,
Waves me hello, he's part of the crowd.
I mimic his moves, in a humorous drill,
We share in the silliness, this wild, green thrill.

As shadows grow long, the moon starts to peek,
A raccoon starts yodeling, the futility's bleak.
In the heart of the night, with mischief aglow,
My laughter erupts; it's a comedy show!

So here in this stillness, I find my delight,
With critters as company, life feels just right.
In the boundless expanse, where no troubles are found,
I embrace this odd world, where laughter is crowned.

www.ingramcontent.com/pod-product-compliance
Lightning Source LLC
Chambersburg PA
CBHW050305120526
44590CB00016B/2491